My Heartbeats
A Book of Poetry By Suzan Johnson

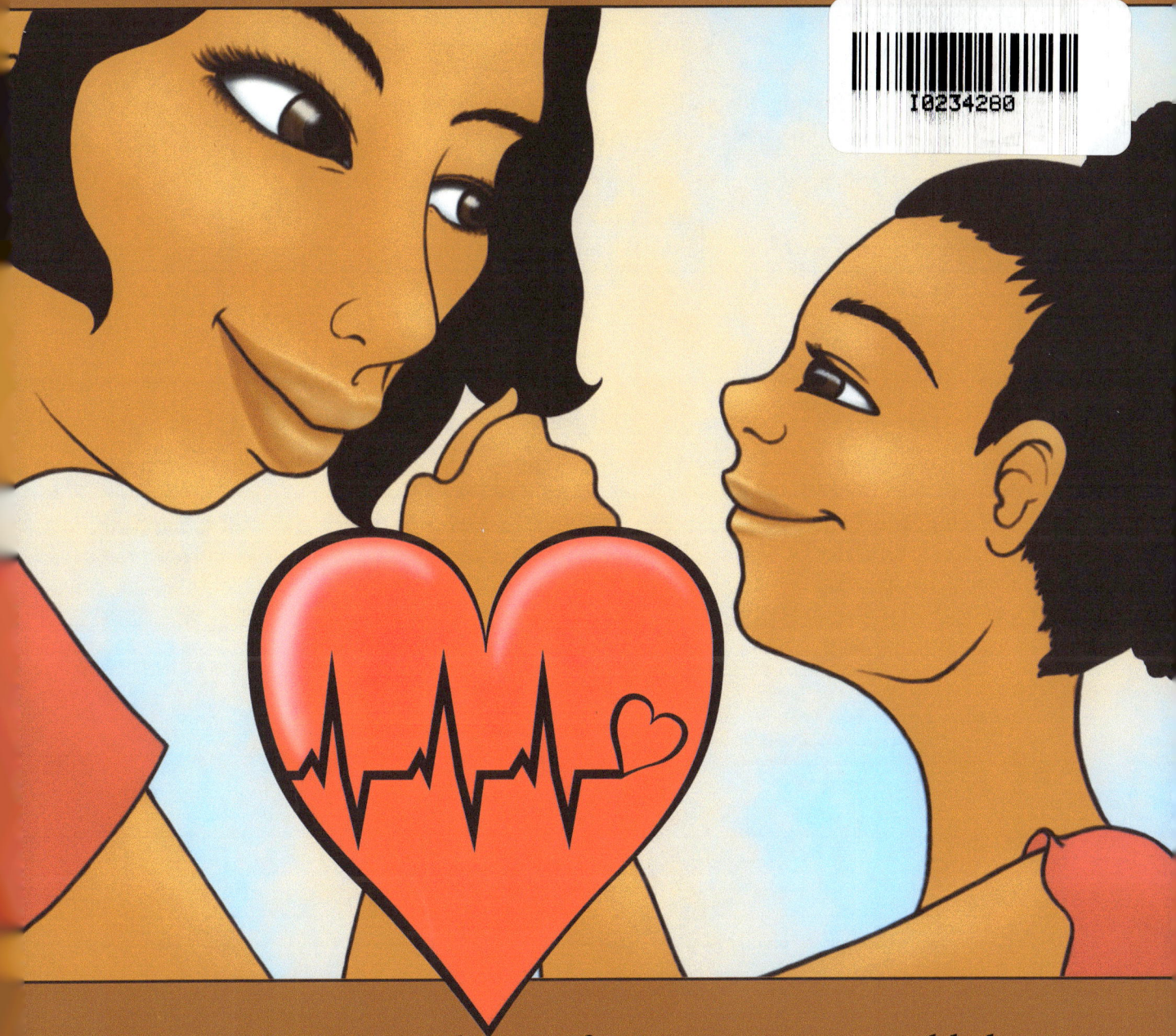

Illustrated by Selina Ahnert of True Beginnings Publishing.
Published by True Beginnings Publishing. Copyright Suzan Johnson, 2015.

ISBN-13: 978-0692594414
ISBN-10: 0692594418

Ordering Information:
To order additional copies of this book, please visit Amazon or shjstories.com.

My Heartbeats
© Suzan Johnson.
First Printing, 2015.

Dedication

This book is dedicated to all of the children who
have been a part of my life.
For those who will enter, I can't wait to meet you.
You are all special to me.

Opening

We often don't tell our loved ones, especially the children in our lives, how we feel about them. I wanted to let a few of my heartbeats know their effect on me. These children have affected my life, and I am forever grateful to their parents for allowing me in.

Flashback

I flashback to you and me in your
Room laughing, talking about my
Dreams, my goals, your dreams,
Your wishes for me.

I flashback to coming home at 11:00pm,
12:00am, 4:00am ... Your room light
Remained on until my bedroom door
Closed...

I flashback to you in the kitchen cooking
Whatever I want, I can see you making me fresh carrot
Juice just the way I like it..."One more
Time in the strainer for me" I say.

I flashback to my college graduation,
I could see the look of pride, and
Love in your Eyes... How I loved that look.

I flashback to feel of your arms around
Me... Nothing else in the world
Compares.

I flashback to our last conversation,
We laughed, and made plans that
Would not come to fruition... "I Love
You" Were the last words I heard you say,
"I love you too" were the last I said to you,
Mom.

Beat, Beat
Descendant of your family's love
Laughing, playing, carefree, and
Effervescent, end exuberant
I know that your future is waiting for you
My Heartbeats

Nat

Dimples, Smiles galore
She cheers, laughs, and dances with glee
Extrovert, and comical indeed
I enjoy hearing her antics and her please to "braid my hair"
Just Nat

On the go

Noting the ups and downs

Eventfully ready to take on the world

Pirouettes galore all by Jadore

Leisurely sharing each other's space

Undeniably the best at what they do

Slam dunks and three pointers by Maddie

One and one

They are both **N**ext in line for greatness

Equals two

Goal

My dream imagines the ball going into the net.
Swoosh past the goalie's hands.
I can wait until Coach puts me in, why not yet?
It's my turn, I dash onto the field
Position myself with heart racing fast.
I grab the ball with my foot, then peer down the field.
It's like a blast from the past.
Last week's game appeared in my head.
I missed the shot.
I feel the dread, "Stop!" I tell myself.

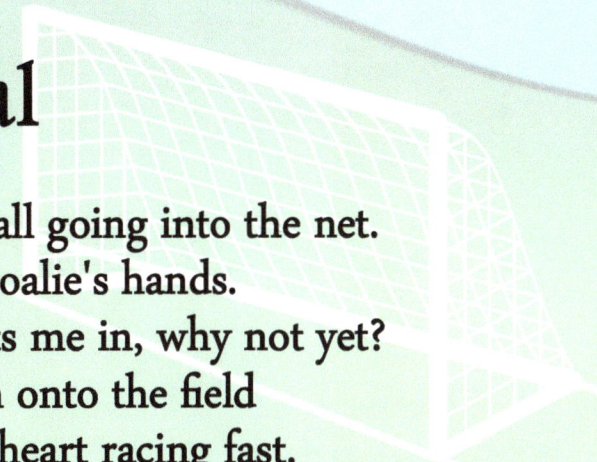

Spirit

I fly high in the air, then I am caught.

The lifts, the toss, they don't seem to end.
I love it!

The practicing, stretching, repeating it over and over again.
I say the words in my sleep, "Go Team!"

Will they hear me? Do the fans hear me?
Do they see me? Do they feel my spirit?

Then we make eye contact.
I fly high in the air, then I am caught.
Go Team!

10

She paints your face with ease.

As her brushes glide, magic takes over.

As a child you dreamed of the fashion,

Glitz, glamor and more.

Clothes, jewelry, design is your heart.

When it is all said and done, no matter your path,

Beauty will always be in your heart.

L ittle lovers of books

I nquistive about my books

Real books are in the nonfiction sec T ion

T ransitioning into chapter books

Reading for the L ove of a good book

E xploring the nooks and crannies of the
bookshelves

Yes, you may have a bookma R k

Molding young minds towards gr E atness

A ble to switch genres at will

D iaries, interviews, and more make up the
biographies

Always tr E at the books with care

Storytime is my favo R ite

My in S piration for working

HARMONY

She's almost never harmonious

Talking, dancing, playing

She keeps smiling with her stories

Rambunctious

"K"

Quietly, your enter, I did not see you come in.
The library welcomes you again.
Your presence is felt before you begin to speak.
I know that smile, I can tell you had a good day.
As we work side by side, we share stories of school,
Home, family, and friends.
There have been TWO of you to come across my path,
TWO who have made me laugh.
I have watched you both grow from little girls to young ladies.
The best is yet come.
I can't wait.

T all buildings

H eightened senses

Cousins through our family tre **E**

C hildren running through the streets

Place of concrete, shows, and
teams you seem to f **I** nd your place

s **T** ories told by my mom of your

adventures

Y ou are never far from my mind

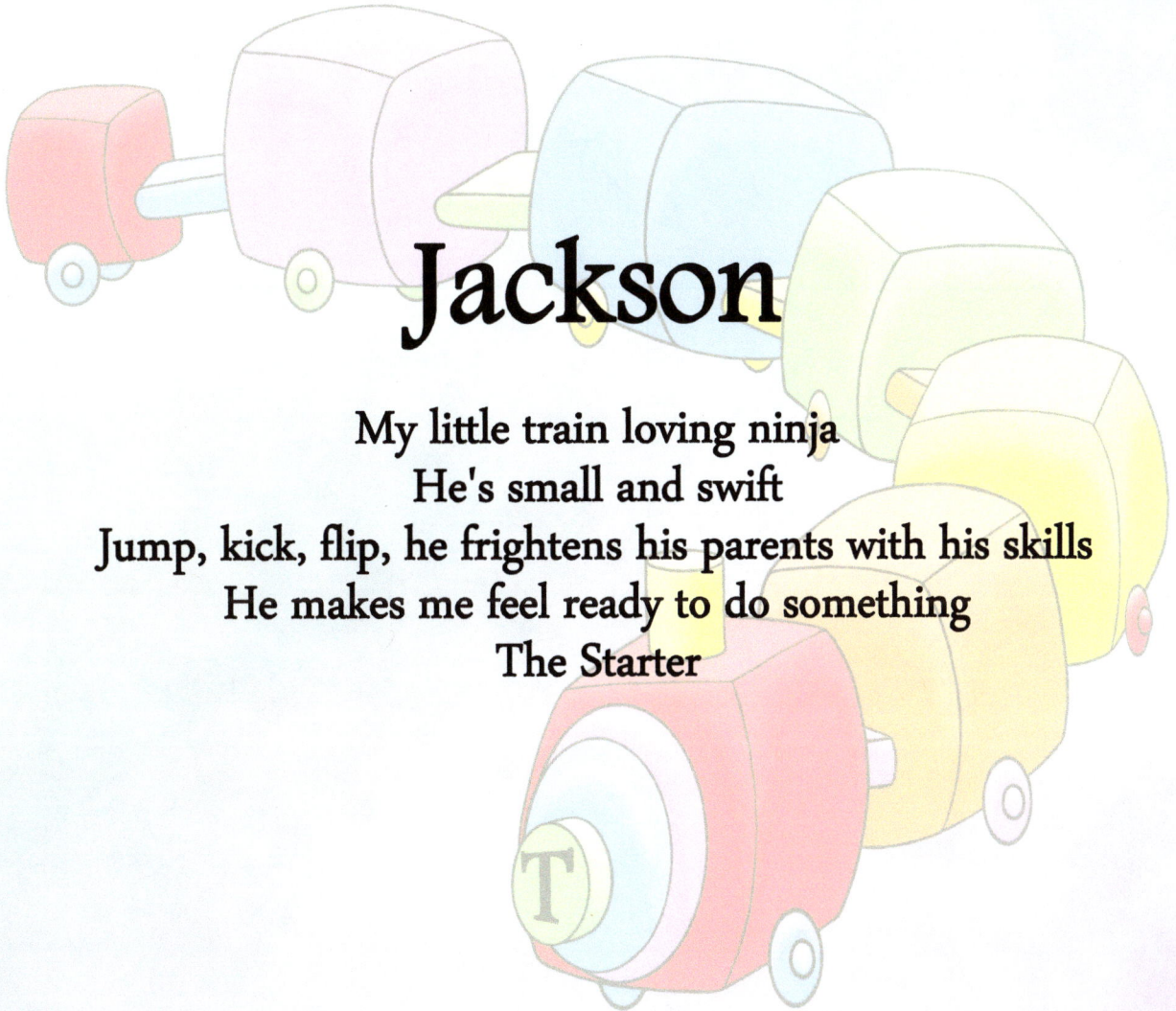

Jackson

My little train loving ninja
He's small and swift
Jump, kick, flip, he frightens his parents with his skills
He makes me feel ready to do something
The Starter

Click, click, click

Smile, stare, Pose, stare

Snap, click, Snap, click

The camera flash is blinding

My best friend and I are going to be stars

Running, Jumping, Breathing

FINISH

At the start
Ready, Set, BOOM!
Off and running, breathe in, breathe out
I can do it, I pass runners with ease until I see numbers 1 thru 3
She may be fast but I am faster, I pull my inner cheetah out
The next gear takes me to another level
Hurdle, jump, run
Hurdle, jump, run
Three more to go and we are side by side
I was born for this
No one can beat me but me
I pass my opponent
Hurdle, jump, run
Hurdle, jump, run
This the most difficult part
I feel my nemesis breathing down my neck
The finish line is in sight
Crossing it will be sweet, don't miss a step
Run, breathe
Run, breathe
The cheers are deafening

The Games

I am lost in a world
Car chases, alien attacks, or epic battles
My mind races through scenarios
How can I win? I need more points
How many lives do I have left?
One more left to go
The Winner, until the next one

Curtain Call

Preparation is key.
Line after line, do I know my part?
I feel the butterflies move
then dance all the way to my beating heart.
The curtain goes up
And "scene", take a bow.

Jessie

Smart beautiful inside and out
Jumping, running, dunking
Oh she thinks she's cute
Learn, give, drive
Young, talented
Jessie

Lili

She has a mischievous smile
Poised and refined
She looks with speaking but never says so much
She makes me feel like she can read my soul
Intuitive

R.J.

Lover of the game
He dibbles, he shoots
I feel exuberance when I think of him
I am sorry that your efforts to teach me have been in vain
The baller handler

Twirl

The music begins
Arms outstretched, body long and lean
I feel the rhythm in my soul
Whirl

Randy

We are from the same place, heart, love, and souls
Nobody knows what we have endured
Left behind with family to mind
No love was lost when we took that flight north
With our group of three
We lived, worked, and loved until one had to leave
We don't always agree but our love is strong
My Brother

More...

Have you always wanted to write your own poems? Well the great thing about poems is they do not have to rhyme. So, check out these great ways to create your own poetry. Remember, poetry is best when shared with others.

Free Verse:

These types of poems can be any length, do not have to rhyme, and they usually follow a topic.

Haiku:

"Haiku" is a traditional form of Japanese poetry. Haiku poems consist of 3 lines. The first and last lines of a Haiku have 5 syllables and the middle line has 7 syllables. The lines rarely rhyme. These poems usually focus on nature.

Line 1: 5 syllables
Line 2: 7 syllables
Line 3: 5 syllables

Acrostic:

An acrostic poem is a poem where certain letters in each line spells out a word or phrase. Typically, the first letters of a line are used to spell the message. But, that rule is not set in stone, the letter can appear anywhere.

A
B
C
D
E
F
G....

April is National Poetry Month, but if you would like to find out more about poetry throughout the year, checkout your school library, local library, and poetry.org.

If you like what you have read,
Please leave a positive review on
Amazon.com or Goodreads.
Thank you!